# *Lets*

# *Take A*

# *Journey*

Logan Gregoire

# *Foreword*

*Picking up from where I had left off it is easy to see how we have all grown. We have become more open about ourselves and about our emotions, with the realization that a lot of us are disconnected from what we truly feel and this is what our struggle has become. We, as a whole, still continue to look through the wrong lens. We continue to fight the wrong battle, instead of taking on our own battle inside, we have continued to go outside and read, or participate in another's war. Technology has become more of an aspect of our lives and cut us off from each other even more. Cut us off from ourselves. Cut us off from the patience and understanding of living amongst others that it is now so easy to become emotional about another person's choice because we have been free to decide what we hear and when we hear it, or read, and how we perceive it.*

*In a world where lost emotions now have control, we need to take a pause. We need to go on a journey of discovery, to find ourselves again. To realize that everything we do will leave an impact, and not just the carbon footprint. The interpersonal footprint that we leave on everyone we interact with, and those who interact with us.*

*In hopes of accomplishing this I have also grown with my poetry, and have opened more up to allow my emotion to come through. I hope that with these words that I have placed in each poem you will feel the emotions, and you will let the words speak to you. Hear the voice in each page, and let it assist you in rediscovering you. All of you.*

*Don't be afraid to say yes, to you. Take a pause, come rediscover what you have lost.*
*Let's take a journey.*

# Table of Contents

“Throw In Your Own Mix”

“A Maniacal Twist"

“How Deep Does It Go?”

“The Power is in the Hair”

“When it’s Finally a (W)rap”

“The Wind, a Page, and a Hand”

“A Towel and a Stone”

“The Sword and the Galaxie”

“All Eyes Off Me”

“Just Slow Down”

“When the Flame Finally Went to Bed”

“The World He Has Unearthed”

“Done With Words”

“I Would've Built Them Upside Down”

“Who is the Real Man of Mystery”

“The Spiral of Doom”

“How One Man Can Light Up a City”

“They Don’t Know What to do With Me”

“When Your Feet Are Locked In”

“Just Let It Unfold”

“Where the Curvatures of the
Atmosphere Meet”

“When You're Ready Open One Eye”

"Your Second Time Around"

"The Great Ring of Towels"

"It's Just a Notebook"

"The Dancing City of Lights"

"The Glow in the Morning"

"As the Auras Come Out"

"When the Mad Man's Back at Work"

"Been Through This Journey Before"

"When There's Lighting Off in the Distance"

"The Work Begins When the Eyes are Closed"

"The Lost Dance"

"The Beauty in Those Eyes"

"Just Jiggle That Brain Matter Around"

"Heaven is On Earth"

"Sprinkle a little dust over it"

"Lets take a Journey"

## "When We Meet the End"

There's just something about this life that You've got to love.
Maybe it's great appreciation for the protection from above,
Possibly even enjoying the flight of a free and elegant dove.

You may adore the light that Only rises in the east,
Or, the subtle things like being thankful for a feast.

This whole world is radiating with so much good.
There's still one concept that is hardly Understood.

Our souls are something that we have to defend,
For on the other side is even more beauty when we meet the end.

## "Sadly Caught Upwind"

It's crazy to think one must be Careful of talking about the wildest aspirations,
As someone is there listening and wanting to bring up previous conversations.
The word they put under Analysis is now turning out to be newly reborn lacerations.

What travels through the air can break almost any piece of mind,
It doesn't take much more than being Under the breeze to create a space redefined,
Then comes a Grueling truth that leaves nothing but the Hard spoken word to hide behind.

It's a feeling that everyone has as if the Times themselves have you pinned,
Even the smallest fire of words can leave people in the smoke where they're sadly caught upwind.

## "When Two Hands Can Craft a World"

It's not that Often when two hands can craft a world into something so beautifully serene,
They can take any lost beauty and lace it with gold for all to be seen.

The hands can take any size twig and turn it into sleeping in comfort,
But they've got to fight hard to maintain their own piece of dirt.

To create such everlasting elegance, it is Not a race,
It just takes putting a little bit of love in the right place.

## "The Power of Now"

Time is something intangible and can't be seen or spent,
So, without a clock there's no Telling where it ever went.

To freeze it would mean becoming a single breath at any given moment.
Now add a conscious thought for the assembly of the final component.

To leave all Others in a state of wow,
One must learn to understand the power of now.

## ""The Only Genuine Reset"

The beauty of balance and order is so delicate that all you have to do is pull one string.
Keep tugging then all of The sudden you've torn apart the whole thing,
Add a spark and you'll see the Horrific devastation that it can all bring.

The flame can transform all bad Examples and make dust of any blood stain.
That terrible thing called want wouldn't even remain,
As everything in its path dwindles down to the softest of grain.

The creation guidelines have already been met,
Now the fire must not be abused as it's the only genuine reset.

## "The Wind and the Flame"

There is unfathomable beauty Found in the story of the wind and the flame.
Starting out very young, playing Inside, from the beginning they knew they weren't the same.
They picked up the tempo, now the house is gone, but who's the one to blame?

The two wanted to stick together through the joyous of good times,
So, they hopped to the next to see if the falling still Rhymes.

They had fun, they danced, and they fought,
They could conquer anything in any given spot.
Now looking back, they Still had just one thought,
If not for each other's existence we would be not.

Neither needed to take a breath so they decided it wasn't worth seeing who's The best.
They eventually went their separate ways to take a heavily needed rest,
And said, "until next time for yet another test."

# "The Beauty of Difference"

The world we live in is crazy and the variety of people is
pretty Vast.
It's why individuals are always competing to not be last.
If we were all the same, every play would have the same cast.

Here we have the beauty of difference that gives us a
phenomenal Array of knowledge on numerous subjects.
Without it, we would all Rely on the same architects,
And then we would be sleeping with even more insects.

With all the personalities of great input there are lots of things
that get accomplished distinctively,
As each person has a natural reaction that they've developed
to do Instinctively.

Now, as everyone takes a subtle look Around,
It's easy to see The elegance of individualism that can be found.

Every conscious person has a set of different Intentions,
And can only be taken on by all of our physical extensions.

There are always plenty Of excuses as to why something wasn't
done a certain way.
Just remember, if there was no difference there would be
absolutely Nothing to say.

# "Just Give 'em That Smile"

There exists a natural grand weapon that provides hope for
anybody to deploy,
While all too Often people are stuck in a mindset of conquer and
destroy.
That intention is unfortunately the exact opposite of what is
needed to create unity and joy.

As we start Finding the ones who want to leave our paths in a
burning pile,
The most inspirational thing to do is just give 'em that smile.
It's the beautiful change the people have needed for a real good
while.

# "No Such Thing as a Bad Child"

You wouldn't understand until you've held one of your own,
A blank slate to the world, where even the parents Themselves have lessons yet to be shown.

The children learn to imitate the walking shadow of our reflections,
Every action we make is Hoisted to their way of life leading them different directions.

Since normal can't Ever be defined, each one of us will always be a crazy, calm, classy, and curious child.
Without the proper guidance the world will continue to get even more wild.

## “Lost In the Days or Lost In the Daze”

Lost in the days or lost in the daze?
Is it More of a question or a phrase?

Are you admiring all the beauty around that’s gratefully mind-blowing in so many ways,
Or are you counting the suns up And down until you can escape living through other people's plays?

Have you been questioning the thought of your own pretty crazy mirage?
It goes, “what was the point of Getting all those expensive toys to just be stuck inside a garage?”

Wouldn’t you rather be a part of the very select few,
Who are Into conquering any element to reach that one breathtaking explicit view?

Some say to be caught in the days is an easy way to avoid committing Crimes,
Others say the daze is for admiring all the grandest of good times.
If you're living inside both, what about each lifestyle rhymes?

## "The Warriors That Didn't Have a Stop"

There are very few who live by the code of the knight.
Bring the kingdom justice, be moral and polite,
Unless there is evil To take care of, just do what's right.
No matter the enemy, never give up in a fight.

Do not hesitate by any opponents type of build,
Even if they appear to be talented and skilled.
The only thing they will Witness is our power of being strong willed.
We have a duty to protect, and It must be fulfilled!

There will be absolutely no fighting for personal gain,
Since we were chosen to Systematically take away other people's pain,
This shall carry on to an even greater cosmic plane.

Honor our ancestors and even Though our bodies will drop,
We will always go down as the warriors that didn't have a stop.

# "Numbers or Superstition"

Are there actually things that live Beyond our sense of sight,
Can they really follow us in the midst of the night?
If it's strong enough, can it truly scratch or bite?

How do we know if the intentions are ever bad or good?
Do we actually receive numbered signs that need to be
better Understood?

Is it true that fear is just airborne,
Or is it just a Thought that is meant to leave us all torn?

Are those feelings just numbers or superstition?
I guess the only way to find out is with your own intuition.

# "You Have Yours and I Have Mine"

You have yours and i have mine.
If we can leave it at that, all Would be fine.
Unfortunately, some people just like to cross that line.

With that being said, you're already on the wrong path,
And you will be the one to Exclusively feel the wrath.

So what don't you understand about what it's like to be nice?
I was patient the first and asked politely twice.
What's your real intention, what View are you willing to sacrifice?
The going rule is, if i ask again it comes with a price.

This is where i say, "i've given you Every chance.
If this is really what you want, it's going to be your last dance.

I am the wielder of time and breath,
If you pull that card... it will be death."

## "What is He Looking Through?"

I was just minding my own business when i heard an Onlooker
ask his friend, "what is he looking through?"
Then the other goes, "don't know but it's got to be magical
because it turns every color then back to blue."
A smirk hit my face and all i could think was, "if only you guys
had the slightest of clue."

You could hear them Noting every single detail,
They were mesmerized as if what i had was from a real-life
fairy tale.

I could tell these weren't the kind of individuals who enjoyed
the Liberty of exploring their curiosity,
So, i approached instead out of my own pure generosity.

At first they were nervous until i asked, "would You like to
have a look?"
You would've thought they got whiplash based on how quickly
their heads shook!

I pulled the mysterious lens from the chain that was around my
neck,
As one glanced through his jaw dropped and out came a
shocked, "oh, what the heck!?"
He handed it to his friend quickly and went, "here, hurry you
give it a check!"

He peeks through and asks, "is it from the future because it
seems to make everything glow?"
I replied, "where it comes from no one will ever know,
It was a gift from a brother that's really good at making people
go whoa!"

# "Fight For Your Center"

There are skills in life which can't be Bought that carry a lot of misconception.
You have to genuinely fight for your center to be able to tap into our own deeper connection.
Only then, can we get Excited for adding these impressive feats to our, "hey check this out!" collection.

To not have a personally diverse unique lineup of tricks,
Would naturally make Gestures towards not understanding the harmonium balance in which our universe ticks.

Sometimes this can involve some not so easy maneuvers with different body parts on the ground,
Then pressing into a shape that can impress all who's around.
This kind of strength is tediously trained Unlike lifting a compressed pound.

There will always be people who say these Notions are unsustainable.
Just remember, some others ideas are nowhere near relatable,
As to achieving the proper balance in life, you better believe you're more than capable.

# "Caught Flipping Through the Pages"

It all began With the thrill of searching for the lost puzzle piece.
Now it's a thought the mind just will not release.

To recall the last place it was seen, has only got me lost.
I hope i didn't leave it on paper with ink that got left out in autumns first frost,
Or, left within the hands of someone who thinks its worthy of getting tossed.

Now think, was it in a dictionary or thesaurus?
Perhaps it was when i heard a soulful melody with an unsung chorus?

I've got full Intention on finding that word i haven't seen or heard in ages,
But i can't remember if it was for calming people's rambunctious outrages.
No, something Tells me it was derived from an ancient spell once cast by mages.
Either way, it's got me seriously stumped and now i'm caught flipping through the pages.

Perhaps it's worth glancing through that mysterious rolodex.
Nope, don't know How anyone can read those kinds of specs.
I just don't understand why everything has to be so complex.

# “What Throws it Off Balance?”

Gather around, it's time for another story.
This comes from my youth, back To the days of glory.

I was always asking questions that no one seemed to understand,
It was apparent the only way to Handle this was resort to the land.

At this point it was time to seek out the great oak.
Legend be told, it was only wisdom he spoke.
He was an old timer and didn’t like being woke.
This being known, i poured out my Emotions then told him a joke.

I began to ask the questions that were oh so big,
His first response was, “take it easy now sprig.
I've done shed a few leaf and broke a couple twig.

A brutal truth you seek, so it seems.
Greater men die for other people's dreams.”

## “Defy the Typical Odds”

Fear... it comes and goes.
Not much different than the way water flows.

It’s typically not an emotion that's ever Sought after,
Why would it? when we'd rather be enjoying each others laughter.

In reality it is just a thought, Perhaps the most challenging game of tug o’ war.
Only because the voice in our head is worried about what happened before.

That’s ay-okay, but life isn't much fun when you take Every safety measure.
At some point you’ve got to have fun and enjoy a little pleasure.

So eventually you have to defy the typical odds inside your mind,
You’d be surprised how much Lost joy you can find.

No sense in being the Loner that goes in a straight line,
I take that back, if you're pushing your limits, then it's all fine.

As to what Simplifies the answer of what it takes to build up some nerve.
Sometimes you just have to sit, watch, and observe,
Take your time, since everyone has a different learning curve.

## "Through a Certain Lens"

Stand for something or be put to rest,
This game of life is more than just a test.

It's through a certain lens you'll see the masses blinded by the light.
Lost and searching for Any answers, with only synthetic epiphanies in sight.

Disconnected from emotions thus becoming greedy,
Consumerism at its peak, people are getting extra Needy.

Signs of yesterday always on repeat,
While there's Demands of everything needing to be complete.

Social status is all just play pretend.
To get to the top, how far will your back bend?

## "The Gear You Brought"

To paint the picture, i was on an adventure with a great comrade.
At the time he definitely wasn't the type to be a restless nomad.
We had only just started a long hike with plenty of conversation to be had.
At one point, he turned to me and asked, "may i be honest with you lad?"
This is where i Nonchalantly nodded and replied, "is it good news or bad?"

The answer i got was, "neither, but we have to take care of business first."
I could tell right away he was focused On quenching his thirst.

He then carried on to say, "i don't know if i should or not,
But i can't help but notice how you look sad over there with the gear you brought."
I interjected right then and said, "now you better hold that thought.
It's apparent to me there's lessons you haven't been taught,
This life isn't about what you've personally bought.
More so who can have fun in any given spot.
So, what do you say we strip all the excess material that you got,
Then let me know When you're ready because i'll show you how to give the real good times a shot!"

# “The Mirror of Force”

It was only a mystery until now, it's what they call the mirror of force.
Rumored to have the secret of life, and its current projected course.

There was a flicker of light, so i Insistently approached, only to realize my eyes were playing a game.
As i got closer, i could see an apparent fault in the mainframe.
I peered in and there was nothing, was i looking through a window pane?
This was supposed to be a mirror, am i starting to go insane?

Suddenly my reflection appeared, and was Testing me to see if i had lost my way.
This left me cold in my tracks. what on earth was i supposed to say?

"How are you talking?" i don't think i could have spoke any faster.
There was a smirk as he said, "the one i am looking upon is the king of disaster.
And the one you see in the mirror is who i call my master.

Now are there any Subjects that you'd like to confess,
The way i see it, you're the one that's a mess.
Would you like to send yourself an s.o.s?

Well, we can't be helped until you're ready to seek change within.
Until then, you'll be sitting around waiting for our story to begin."

# "A Journey of Words"

When it comes to people, each individual carries their own ability To be freed,
As the world is on the verge of falling victim to an unknown individual's greed.
Now we're trained to Imitate each other as if we forgot the name of our own breed.

Who would have ever thought the use of language could be such a slippery slope?
Especially, when you embark on journey of words to bring back the inspiration and a lost thing called hope.

So how does one make any Movement on what proves to be a deadly chess board?
It starts with mustering up some courage and harnessing a finely tuned vocal chord.

With the right words in order, it is possible to reunite an entire nation.
As the people will eventually quit Eluding their problems and embrace positive transformation.

A journey of words awaits so take careful notes or you just might lose track.
Now each page contains a message with an even deeper code to crack,
To get the final results, you'll have to file twice through this whole stack.

## "Throw In Your Own Mix"

We've all been there, sitting at a set of cross roads.
Torn between choices, just hoping courage loads.

It's never really the greatest place To be,
Instead of two options, naturally there's three.

One path is simple, stick to tradition.
Just blend in where there's no competition,
Or, take a different route to evolve into a new edition.

There's only one Other way to truly cure the madness,
It's a matter of letting go of all the things you'll miss.
Then blaze a new trail and say, "i got this."

Since no two worlds are ever the same,
There's always a different picture inside every frame.

The internal battle is one of the hardest conflicts.
Eventually, you just have to throw in your own mix.

## "A Maniacal Twist"

There was a day when i was out playing in the mist.
Things really changed as i reached the other side and there it was,
a maniacal twist!
I had stumbled across a land the People called the wild west,
It was a barren landscape where i knew i was just a guest.

All the views were astonishingly new!
I couldn't believe my eyes as the tumbleweeds blew.
Up in the skies is where the vultures flew,
And somewhere in the hills the bandits were Lurking as a crew.

I had explored a little more As i got to see the wild horses run.
Lessons were learned like, don't walk into a saloon without a gun,
Or interrupt a rancher while he's on a cattle run.

This was the furthest thing from ever being bland,
To see nature in the purest beauty was oh so grand!
As i returned i was told, "You now know what it's like to see all
infrastructure be returned back to sand."

# "How Deep Does It Go?"

To solve the great question, i once gave it a try.
It seems most will carry on until their blood runs dry.
Even i can't tell what intention lies behind the flicker of another person's eye.

I wish i could say the light on the other side of that mountain was the sunrise.
It's really just an aura of all the city's misfortune, corruption, and lies.
It won't ever go out until they can Withdraw all the people's cries.

So how does raw emotion create such an Incredibly bright light?
Well, it starts with individuals being selfish and wanting everything in sight.

It doesn't matter the color of their work collar,
They all stretch themselves Thin trying to harvest a dollar.

As for the answer, we will Honestly never know,
How deep does it go?

## "The Power is in the Hair"

In this world there are some people who just don't care,
So i'm going to say it outright, the power is in The hair.

You don't need words or material to get unspoken respect.
Just make sure your hygiene doesn't leave signs Hinting towards self neglect.

It's a tough world and Exhaustion can kick your butt.
Don't let others opinions put you in a rut,
Keep being you and owning that unique strut.

# "When it's Finally a (W)rap"

While others are out there talking about sticks and stones,
I've focused my intention on how a word Makes rhythm without tones.

Since then, i can say i have constructed something that is quite unique.
Instead of playing It, it's a word hide and seek.
It'll make your head Spin, so take a closer peek.

I got riddles To be written,
Rather old bars to be spittin'.

Just know when it's finally a (w)rap,
You would have fallen into the word trap.

# "The Wind, a Page, and a Hand"

Everything was still on a calm cloudy day,
When the wind decided it wanted to come out and play.
It looks like the weather already has an Outline of what it wants to say.

Out on the mountain was a notebook flipped to an empty page,
And the hand of a creator who knew it was a very Unique stage.

It was obvious that something like this will never occur again,
This exact moment is what changed the dancing tempo of a pen.

The gusts got stronger and evolved from a breeze,
Now it was time to listen to the whispering of the trees.

They said, "stop the Trembles, if you can manage,
Use the change of the winds to your advantage.

This may all sound very strange,
But it is possible to be one step ahead of change."

## “A Towel and a Stone”

I heard a voice from Within say, “come back to the wild,
Things are a little different now that you’ve grown from a child.
This time you have to leave everything behind that you’ve gathered and compiled.”

At first i was scared as i Intensely thought,
You mean, i have to disregard everything i bought?

With such a crazy world, it's going to be Tough,
I'll bring just two things, that should be enough.
Afterall, this journey just might get a little rough.

Right away i snagged up a towel and a stone,
These two things can get me anywhere, even when out alone.

Now, it was time to conquer the lands.
With these two tools and a good pair of Hands,
I knew anything could be built out there in the sands.

At this point, i didn’t know what challenges mother nature was going to throw,
Nor was i concerned, for there's nothing better than the places you'll go...

# "The Sword and the Galaxie"

"Okay, hold on. let me get this straight.
You mean to tell me i'm here to defend the word that They all call fate?
Doesn't that seem like a bit much to put on one humans plate?"

The great then spoke, "you've already come this far, are you really going to be scared?
Would your attitude be different if i said i don't think you would even if dared?

Now quit acting like you were raised by fools,
Let me at least Help you by giving you a couple tools."

It was in this moment a sword and a galaxie was uncovered,
The two most powerful things that have ever been discovered.

"I know your resume states that you can already weave the sands,
But i've still got to warn you of the power when these two items are wielded in the hands.
They have the ability to Extinguish the future as well as these lands.

You've been chosen as the warrior to guard all the stars in our universe.
Unfortunately, it's not a position that we can prep you for or rehearse,
It's with these two weapons i'm sure you'll know what to do when matters take a turn for the worse."

## "All Eyes Off Me"

I'm on a dangerous mission to set the people free,
The opposition says, "hope is Outdated kid, just let it be."
They know i carry truth that the great Leaders don't want you to see.
All while false accusations keep coming and the system Demands a plea.

One thing is for certain, i'm going to keep doing me.
If you want to help, keep all eyes off me.

## "Just Slow Down"

Sometimes when you're cruising and there isn't Anybody around,
All you want to do is hear that awesome rumbling sound!

It's a sure fire way to get blood pumping through the vein,
When you crack it full throttle down a wide open lane!
Hitting speeds that'll make someone question whether or Not
you've gone insane.

It's always a delight to tango between the lines,
But nobody ever likes paying those hefty fines.

So if you don't want your smile to be Diluted into a frown,
You have to remember as you approach the next town.
All you got to do is, just slow down.

## “When the Flame Finally Went to Bed”

Nature knew it was time for a reset,
The upcoming season was going to be a threat.

It was about time for her to release some rage,
She set the land in flames to begin a new stage.

After all this time, it was a pretty good run.
Now, leaves are Internally burning like the colors of the sun.

Secretly this is all fueled with a hidden desire.
Give each leaf flight to cover the world in falling fire.

Eventually, every last piece of green will be embered,
Leaving the branches empty, Now with nothing left to be remembered.

From these ashes a new phoenix will rise,
Growing even stronger for a more beautiful surprise.

## “The World He Has Unearthed”

At first he thought the world he has unearthed was only just a myth.
Turns out the others weren't lying about the devastation that he Will have to work with.

The land that lays before him was left in fire and smoke,
Previous beings had left nature completely burnt and broke.

It left him in awe as he was Intently staring with a raised eyebrow.
He couldn’t believe how someone could have done this, he didn’t know how.
Best thing to do is get to work now.

At first he said, “i Think i’ll give the people a new voice of reason.
Learn to respect the beauty of each and every season.

Next is the step where i plant a bunch of new seeds,
This should be enough to cover a large variety of needs.

Now what about a power source so that there isn't a need for any excessive mining?
That right there, would be an exponential silver lining.

I guess the only thing left is to figure out How to turn the lights back on,
This would give at least half a day where all darkness is gone."

## "Done With Words"

The things i write about aren't just childish rhymes,
These words are here for the people to get through some hard times.

You see, at one point i used to have a seamless flow.
Now, i feel as if i'm Trapped in an endless burrow,
Because i broke modern language, so where on earth did it go?

Anymore these days, i'm just Hoping things start to make scents.
But all my words are twisted, now it doesn't make any sense.
I was told to get through this i have to use my common cents.

Don't even get me started on the words weird or wired.
By the time i'm done explaining i will have probably already retired.
Hopefully by the time you read this Each and every one of you are somewhat inspired.

I'm done with words, and i don't what is dew,
It's time for me to find something that has been long over do.
If i can't find language in time, i won't know what to due.

## “I Would've Built Them Upside Down”

Lets face it, how they were built we haven't the slightest clue.
Oh boy, would it be cool to see what they looked like when they were New!

The pyramids scattered around the world are mesmerizing and really blow my mind,
There's just something that bothers me about how they were designed.

If it were my choice, i would've built them upside down,
They'd have the most intricate shadows casting across the ground.
I'd design the proper angles to let the winds have their
own Expression as they make their own sound.

There would be certain algorithms to make it seamlessly flow.
The light from above Wow's, as each day there's a new show.

For it to tell the same story would take another go around the sun,
That's just the beginning of what i consider fun!

Now many are thinking would that just collapse?
Well that's the world of what if's, so it just might, perhaps.

Inside i would create a new language where you have to know the art of translation.
Once it's understood, you will know what it takes to make the greatest transformation.

## "Who is the Real Man of Mystery"

Out there is a man doing work that is ever so faint.
We don't know who he is yet, Hopefully he's a saint.

Rumor has it that he is the one and only mid-knight.
Fighting between our days, chasing After the lost light.

With powers beyond our realm, he can push Today's wind.
Jumping between dimensions where reality has thinned.

He carries the keys to a galaxie, with an all the access pass to the matrix.
Cruising through the universe into Tomorrow, where times rusty ratchet clicks.

As he passes by Each moment, the dust of eternity is never seen again.
Taking everything with him including future, present, and then.

Upon his return down the Road he will dress the sky in black.
So that he can tell the moon and stars another wise crack.

One of the greatest questions in history,
Will always be, who is the real man of mystery?

# "The Spiral of Doom"

Everything in this universe Focuses on continually spinning around.
Thankfully, there's an atmosphere around this rock that keeps us On the ground,
And a genetic code that allows us to be identified and found.

There wouldn't be an issue if we all had the same concept of long term sustainability,
But the majority of people have lost the idea of genuine humility.
Now there are greater repercussions that take away from the natural tranquility.

The spiral of doom has led to ignorance of negative generational repetitions.
Now there exists an unwanted double helix with too many faulty acquisitions,
As nature creates greater rotating forces for the Replenishment of people without greedy addictions,
To create a world of difference with much better intentions.

## “How One Man Can Light Up a City”

He cheers others up With a smile and doesn’t accept defeat.
You see, he is just a normal guy who knows we all have to make ends meet,
Along with everyone else who roams the endless concrete.

All too often he comes across people who say this life just blows,
But he knows he can change their day with the simplest of Hello’s.

He sees through what is considered modern day success,
It's always been a way of making people an emotional mess.
With this knowledge he isn't ever concerned about what's in the press.

This is why he makes gestures towards others to let them know that they are seen,
And reminds them that there's a whole world out there waiting for them, Even without a screen.

To not live a life of joy and happiness is really just a pity.
It's truly just the simple things, Now that’s how one man can light up a city.

# "They Don't Know What to do With Me"

I know why they don't know what to do with me,
They are the Individuals who know how to look, not how to see.

I don't sit around to watch time pass,
I take lessons from the hourglass.

I believe in truth; they believe in fact.
The fewer the words the greater the impact.

## "When Your Feet Are Locked In"

Every action and choice made means it's time for another unknown ride.
This brings on many more options that lead to catastrophe if we don't quickly decide,
Then naturally of all things, you're caught slipping in the slide.
The moment will quickly test if you're the real master of this kind of stride,
Or if you happen to Portray the false image of maintaining a casual glide.

At this point, it's not time to worry about all that could be Lost,
As beforehand there was Ambitions on doing it at any cost.

Since there has been nothing bad to happen Yet.
When your feet are locked in for the next set,
Would you be willing to take that bet?

## "Just Let It Unfold"

Problems are always lurking, even before you Wiggle out of bed.
So don't go looking for trouble, it will find you instead.

Put out the smokes and set down the beer,
It's time to shift this life into high gear.

Everyone has potential and greatness within,
The hardest part is figuring out just where to begin.

With a lost sense of focus and a want to explore,
Don't know where the journey will take you? best start Inching towards the door.

Stay on your Toes and avoid any expectations.
Premeditated thought can lead to serious complications.

Rushing through everything can eventually turn into a crime,
It seems to begin with not properly Honoring time.

At this point, truth be told,
All you have to do, is just let it unfold.

# “Where the Curvatures of the Atmosphere Meet”

Let me take you to a place where Time doesn’t exist.
Into the skies we go, where storms are still particalized mist.

Along the ride up, you'll see where the curvatures of the atmosphere meet.
There's nothing that Heals a soul faster than when the clouds are at their feet.

First timers will experience an Existential crisis as they open up the door.
Adrenaline kicks in as they scoot closer to the exit where it's just them and the ground floor.

Reaching terminal velocity is what separates being in a freefall or having the ability to fly.
Once that canopy opens up, you'll miss the Solitude of the sky.

Altitude is your best friend, Especially in a skydive,
There's really no other place that will make you feel as alive.

# "When You're Ready Open One Eye"

What am i to do, When i lost my pride?
With all this built up darkness inside,
This is going to be one hell of a ride.

There's got to be something that will help me cope.
Guess i'll keep Ordering drinks until i've found some hope.

It's about that time to line up some Rows of shots,
Allow myself to dive deep into the origins of my thoughts.

I learned that the heavier the tip the heavier the hand.
Realized i'm mad because of what they're Doing to the land.

Even noticed i'm more scared of what i can become.
I've shut myself out from me, thus living numb.

At some point i have to do Something to face the flames,
Instead of sitting here playing my own mind games.

Well i've now wasted all this time spent under the weather,
It's about to be the moment where i pull myself together.

With that said... different poem, different state.
We all got the same problems, so i can relate.

## “Your Second Time Around”

Now to think what happened last time... ahh i remember!
There was rushing winds through the pines in the cold of novemeber.

Those were the days when i Intuitively thought everything was a race.
Lessons have been learned, now i have no need to hide a poker face,
Because the scars show that i'm the craziest one in this place.

It's time to do this again but show how much i care.
Go give it a bit of style and a magical flair,
Since there's no better time as these new pages are unwritten and bare.

We’re gonna treat this chapter like a piece of glass.
This isn't the kind you just see and pass,
It has the capability of competing in any class.

Time to get up and kick some dust up off the ground.
There's potential out there To craft the most harmonious sound,
Or write hidden codes for the greats to be found.
One thing is for sure, the outlook is different your second time around.

## "The Great Ring of Towels"

I don't have a big brain, i just think too much.
With all these broken words, i could Justify needing a mental crutch.

Just so happens i know a guy that knows a guy,
He can take you somewhere Unusual, if you're willing to try.

The great ring of towels is where i chose to go,
Where i can finally take things nice and slow,
Process my ideas and allow myself to grow.

With so many thoughts on different Stances, i started to make a list.
If it was the same page we were on, consciousness would have no purpose to exist.

Old wisdom doesn't come without youthful curiosity,
That's why direction Tells the difference between speed and velocity.

So different we are not, it's unique i choose to be.
This single thought is what will set you free.

My time was about up and i didn't want to leave.
It's best to enjoy the moment, then take time to grieve.

I told this place it's never a goodbye, only a see you later,
For we are all destined to be something greater.

## "It's Just a Notebook"

A gentleman once approached me walking a certain type of way,
The type of walk that states, "i'm not here to play."
It only made me more curious on What he had to say.

He came out with the accusation of a very absurd claim,
Carrying a bark from the Others that said i was to blame!
I replied, "you're wasting your time playing their game,
We haven't even exchanged a single first name."

It was hard to fathom the interpersonal traits he had groomed with so much Neglect.
I said, "try again, please, but with at least a little bit more respect."

He then expressed why he had To trek all the way across the land,
It was an attempt to figure out what i was holding in my hand.
I said, "only the greatest ideas to change the world and be oh so mighty grand!

Now if you'll notice you were quick on the assumptions and my hand you never shook.
I've got better things to do than to be a stranger's appointed crook,
And this thing i have right here, it's just a notebook."

## "The Dancing City of Lights"

I was once granted access to the dancing city of lights.
You could spend a lifetime exploring all the extraordinary sights!
It will always go down as one of the best you'll never forget kind of nights.

As i was approaching i heard something say, "this must be your first time surely,
All we ask it that you behave Maturely."

I had to really think Analytically on why there was a voice coming from the skies.
Then it dawned on me, that the lenses on the roof were covering hidden eyes.

It was the least of my worries since there was so much to be seen.
First, i wanted to Test out that fancy light up machine!
While approaching a gentleman said, "careful, that thing will wipe your pockets clean."

After a while i wanted To wander around the streets,
I couldn't believe the amount of people out performing what seemed to be impossible feats.

There were places you could Enter a double sliding door.
Inside was an outstandingly well dressed person who would ask you,"what floor?"
All i could think to myself was, "wait you mean to tell me there's more!?"

It was as if this place was forever expanding,
Out on other streets were people holding signs that read "Righteousness is demanding!"
On another was an elegant water display that was majestically dancing.

At the end of the night there was a room where we all stood in silence and oddly bid each other a farewell.
If anybody ever asks what happened, i'll just smile and say, "the rule is once you leave, there are some things you just cannot tell."

## “The Glow in the Morning”

There was a period where i spent many nights up in the comfort of a well aged willow.
I was most grateful to experience having a piece of mother nature as my pillow.

The tree itself Now is much more than a century old,
Oh, how i could tell you about all the stories she told!
One that always sticks out is what she said when i was cold.

"You know, even a star's light gets lost in space.
Soon there will be a glow in the morning that warms up the whole place.
Afterall, you are the Only one who can decide which feelings you choose to trace.

Now, you can let outside elements affect your thoughts to a new level of severity,
Or think like the Winners and focus on the beauty to find some mental clarity."

## "As the Auras Come Out"

We all have a different way of singing the blues.
If you can't Tell, a lot of us are good at hiding the clues.

Now, we walk amongst the population as if our internal light has been stolen.
No need to be down, we can still ignite the fire from a few embers that are rollin'.

All it takes is a bit of fuel and just one spark,
To take your life back and escape from the dark.

Once you light the flame, all the Others will know.
As the auras come out, they see a whole different glow.
Now it's time to shine! afterall, this is your show.

# “When the Mad Man's Back at Work”

There are things in this world that are absolutely foreseeable.
It's for too many rookies of the arts to craft things that are unheard and indistinguishable,
Now it's time to Do something remarkably unbelievable.

Placed before you is extravagant magic hidden in disguise!
That’s because Everything is dedicated to inspiring the people for that once in a lifetime prize.

Here’s where all the intentions are placed Carefully for that one special part,
This is the proper way to deliver meaningful words right In the center of the heart.

Every thought that is vocalized comes with some
serious Preparation.
Afterall, this the greatest way to receiving the utmost
of admiration,
As this is only the second part to the application.

Things get pretty serious when there's words and phrases
that are Handling increasingly hefty weight,
It will leave Even the greatest mind in a questionable mental state.

The times seem as if they get Rougher since were trapped living through yesterday's tomorrow where everything is berserk,
But the most indescribable things happen when the mad man's back at work.

## "Been Through This Journey Before"

They said "the Tempests are coming, you better run in fear!"
Well i've been through this journey before, so lets have some fun, go grab your gear.

Too many people are worried about if they're going to suddenly die,
You see, we're the type of Humans that get wild with a y.

Yes, there are times when a good idea fails.
There's no point in sitting around nervous, just to bite your nails.
I can show you an Example of how to properly set your sails.

We've hit the ground hard, but there's no sense in dwelling on a bad crash.
This life's too short and it'll be gone in a flash.

I wouldn't let a lost Society tell you that your actions are too dangerous.
Everybody has different limits and you yourself knows when it's time to get serious.

Now we are the individuals who tend to live life a little risky.
At the end of Every day we can sit around the table, have a few good laughs, and maybe sip on some fine whiskey.

# "When There's Lighting Off in the Distance"

I remember back to the rolling cornfields in the brisk winds of fall,
There was a small acreage on the gravel with a beautifully aged brick wall.
When storms brewed in the distance, it had the greatest view of them all!

One day i was hanging out with a family member of a younger Year.
The skies out west weren't looking the slightest bit clear,
To see dark clouds light up was his only biggest fear.
I said, "if that's the case, come on Over here."

He was terrified as i pointed to the Upcoming thundering on the land.
I began with telling him to listen as we are in the presence of mother nature's greatest band.
Knowing i'd have to further elaborate for him to understand.

We sat and watched in silence as the harmonic symphony was played,
I then made further Remarks on why not to be afraid.
This was one of his life changing moments, Entailing a newer man being made.

There's always a way to bring new light to anybody's existence,
Any moment can be used such as when there's lighting off in the distance.

# "The Work Begins When the Eyes are Closed"

Without the ability to dance through trouble with Grace,
Frustrations will build as you get more red in the face.

Then, when that one problem becomes plural,
It pushes you Over the edge into a mind swirl.

With all that bottled up inside, there's a very strange feeling.
A gut reminder of Needing internal healing.

Running from everything only creates Nests for drama,
It doesn't take long to evolve into full blown trauma.

No more evading the problems inside your mind,
There's still a few pieces of you we Absolutely need to find.

The work begins when the eyes are closed.
Once you're there, the secret can be exposed.

Something magical happens when those tears finally hit the ground,
Mental chains are broken as you and pain are no longer bound.

# "The Lost Dance"

As a single lost soul dances like Nobody is around in the shade,
They shed the colors that once brought its beautiful shine down to a fade.
It's after the last expressive movement a whole new being is made.

The wind blows Ever so gently, right through the crisp air.
Then takes those faded energy shards and leaves them on the ground blank and bare.

This resets the mind as if it had taken a fancy magical potion,
But the reality was letting it all out in expressive motion.
After the transformation the dancer Expects to proceed with nothing less than absolute devotion.

It can erase the thought of a broken romance,
And allow the being to be motivated for yet another chance,
If one can partake in what is considered to be the lost Dance.

## "The Beauty in Those Eyes"

There are times when elegance is misleading from the start.
This is where the deceptive trickery has only begun to show its art.

Often times intentions are never good As this hinders the ability to grow,
Since the user knows how to manipulate emotion and turn it into their own show.

Anyone's soft gaze is capable of covering even the ugliest disguise.
Now some would consider this is a gentle word from the wise,
Always be careful when it comes to falling in love with the beauty in those eyes.

# "Just Jiggle That Brain Matter Around"

Huh? something about Being smart?
Sorry, i must have missed that part.
You see i'm the kind of guy to giggle at a fart.

I was told to be normal, but the Initial thought of that really blows,
Anymore these days i like to get stupid with two o's!
However, there are other times where my foolishness really shows.

You ever play the Game where you say everything with a slur?
It's pretty simple, you just act like you drank too much liquor.

The word that holds the most Glory is city,
Because it gives you a free pass to say things like shitty.

What about the one where you shake your head
until you Eventually hear a sound?
That's the one i call, just jiggle that brain matter around.

Some people would say, "dude that's not Right."
It doesn't really matter, because i carry a smile all night,
And i've got to be the happiest guy anywhere in sight!

## "Heaven is On Earth"

It's sad to think most People won't ever see it, because of the way they say their i's.
Heaven is on earth and each day is a prize.
If you don't believe me, you should experience a cotton candy sunrise.

Even with this truth many will still Let it all burn,
Until they discover their final hour where they're actually willing to learn.

This is a magical place, where All dreams can come true,
The sky can storm in any color, and with a rainbow it returns blue.

Happiness around here isn't something that is just Ticking away.
Many a people just forgot what it's like to see the beauty gifted each day.

Upon night fall there's all those stars to play connect the dots,
Where we can escape reality and Time to slow down the incomplete thoughts.

Just about when you've seen it all, the clouds Enter a sequence that turn from crimson red, to violet, then white.
Leaving us forever questioning what happens when our term is up with this vessel as it enters that tunnel of light.

Well, i'm going to say it again because this place is the best.
Earth is where we come to heaven to take that final Rest.

# “Sprinkle a Little Dust Over It”

"Lets Take a Journey"

# The
# Next
# Chapter
# is
# Yours...

www.ingramcontent.com/pod-product-compliance
Lightning Source LLC
Chambersburg PA
CBHW062142280426
43673CB00072B/123
*9781935821670*